HAL•LEONARD
INSTRUMENTAL
PLAY-ALONG

AUDIO
ACCESS
INCLUDED

PLAYBACK+
Speed • Pitch • Balance • Loop

CELLO

Disney
FROZEN II

Audio arrangements by Peter Deneff

To access audio visit:
www.halleonard.com/mylibrary

"Enter Code"
5591-4826-1875-8559

Disney Characters and Artwork © 2019 Disney

ISBN 978-1-5400-8383-8

HAL•LEONARD®

For all works contained herein:
Unauthorized copying, arranging, adapting, recording, Internet posting, public performance,
or other distribution of the music in this publication is an infringement of copyright.
Infringers are liable under the law.

Visit Hal Leonard Online at
www.halleonard.com

Contact us:
Hal Leonard
7777 West Bluemound Road
Milwaukee, WI 53213
Email: info@halleonard.com

In Europe, contact:
Hal Leonard Europe Limited
42 Wigmore Street
Marylebone, London, W1U 2RN
Email: info@halleonardeurope.com

In Australia, contact:
Hal Leonard Australia Pty. Ltd.
4 Lentara Court
Cheltenham, Victoria, 3192 Australia
Email: info@halleonard.com.au

ALL IS FOUND

CELLO

Music and Lyrics by KRISTEN ANDERSON-LOPEZ
and ROBERT LOPEZ

© 2019 Wonderland Music Company, Inc.
All Rights Reserved. Used by Permission.

SOME THINGS NEVER CHANGE

CELLO

Music and Lyrics by KRISTEN ANDERSON-LOPEZ
and ROBERT LOPEZ

© 2019 Wonderland Music Company, Inc.
All Rights Reserved. Used by Permission.

INTO THE UNKNOWN

CELLO

Music and Lyrics by KRISTEN ANDERSON-LOPEZ
and ROBERT LOPEZ

© 2019 Wonderland Music Company, Inc.
All Rights Reserved. Used by Permission.

Slower

Moderately

LOST IN THE WOODS

CELLO

Music and Lyrics by KRISTEN ANDERSON-LOPEZ
and ROBERT LOPEZ

Moderate Ballad, in 2

© 2019 Wonderland Music Company, Inc.
All Rights Reserved. Used by Permission.

THE NEXT RIGHT THING

CELLO

Music and Lyrics by KRISTEN ANDERSON-LOPEZ
and ROBERT LOPEZ

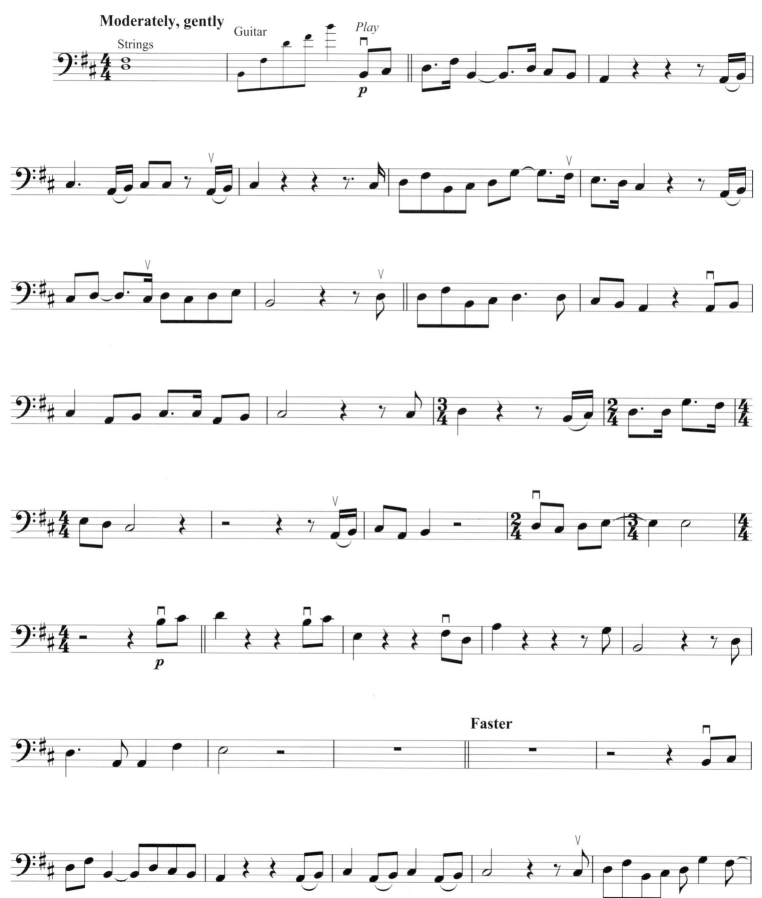

© 2019 Wonderland Music Company, Inc.
All Rights Reserved. Used by Permission.

REINDEER(S) ARE BETTER THAN PEOPLE (CONT.)

CELLO

Music and Lyrics by KRISTEN ANDERSON-LOPEZ
and ROBERT LOPEZ

SHOW YOURSELF

© 2019 Wonderland Music Company, Inc.
All Rights Reserved. Used by Permission.

WHEN I AM OLDER

CELLO

Music and Lyrics by KRISTEN ANDERSON-LOPEZ
and ROBERT LOPEZ

© 2019 Wonderland Music Company, Inc.
All Rights Reserved. Used by Permission.